SHEBOYGAN OCCASIONS

poems by

Lisa Vihos

EST 2024

Lone Snake Editions

SHEBOYGAN , WISCONSIN

Sheboygan Occasions
Lone Snake Editions © 2025
Lisa Vihos

ISBN: 979-8-218-78727-1

Published in the United States of America

Lone Snake Editions
Sheboygan, Wisconsin

Cover and book design by Water's Edge Press

Cover Image by the author: Magnetic Bottle Cap pictures made by visitors to the Midsummer Festival of the Arts in 2021 at the John Michael Kohler Arts Center. Each cap holds an image decorating a word in the poem "Acrostic for Ruth DeYoung Kohler."

Author photo by Michael Hoover

To Sheboygan, Malibu of the Midwest

Introduction

One of the greatest joys of being a poet laureate has been the opportunity to write occasional poems. Not infrequent poems, but rather, poems written upon request for special occasions. During my five years as Sheboygan's first poet laureate (2020-2025), I had requests for poems from three mayors, a judge, the John Michael Kohler Arts Center, various community groups, and a dance company.

This book pulls together that batch of poems, along with other poems that I wrote for occasions of my own: for projects at schools, in response to COVID, and poems in praise of moments and places—some joyful, some sorrowful—specific to my life in Sheboygan.

I moved to Sheboygan with my family in 2002 and have lived here longer than any other place in my life. I hope that taken as a whole, this collection of poems will provide someone who is not from Sheboygan with a picture of this place in every season. And, if you are lucky enough to live in this lovely city by the lake, I hope you will see something here that you recognize as home.

Lisa Vihos
September 5, 2025

Contents

SHEBOYGAN
OCCASIONS

Sheboygan, Our City

From smokestacks to steeples,
our city holds onto itself
around a river that pours into a lake,
a great lake.

From bridges to piers
our city works to find connections
as students make their way to school
and coffee shops bustle open.

From chairs to cheese
from children to churches,
our city has a long history
steeped in art and industry.

From one choir to another,
our city sings to itself every morning
and every evening, the voices rising
like clouds billowing in a blue, blue sky.

Our city has at least two sisters,
one day, maybe more: Tsubame in Japan
and Esslingen in Germany. When we gather
with our sisters, it is always a joyful reunion.

Our city is built on the traditional
homelands of the Ho-Chunk,
Potawatomi, Menominee, Oneida,
and Ojibwe people

along the southwest shores of Michigami,
that lake, that great lake that is our mother.
We respect all who came before us, all
who live with us, and all those yet to come.

Our city is a beautiful place
full of kind and caring people
who represent it, govern it, protect it
and share it with each and every one.

For the swearing in ceremony of Mayor Ryan Sorenson, April 15, 2025

May Each One Flow

From morning dew to evening rain,
     water blesses the fields,
          makes all things green.

         Soil yearns for moisture
    and by water's touch
new life comes, prepares the harvest.

From silent spring to rushing stream
     nutrients move, fish spawn,
         and all is given.

        Life is the river we carry unseen.
    May each one flow to the great lake,
clear and clean.

At the request of Chris Frederickson, Mayor of Rhinelander, 2018-2021

Generosity's Gift

Life is a process not forged alone
but made in time by many hands.
From fire and water to blood and bone,
each in our way, we come to stand.

Just as the tree with branches tall
spreads its roots in soil deep,
providing shade to each and all
and hummingbirds a place to sleep.

For beauty lies in toil unseen
and transformation leads to grace.
Beneath this canopy of green
so many pillars hold this place.

Even when our bodies fail
and we release this earthly load,
our seeds live on and joy sets sail
in deeds well done and gifts bestowed.

*For the John Michael Kohler Art Center's unveiling of the Sandy Sachse
Gratitude Fountain, June 1, 2024*

March Villanelle

Morning sun sparkles on melting snow
and birds are chirping. Must be a sign
that March is here. Let winter go!

Take care when walking on icy floes,
wear proper boots and you'll be fine.
Morning sun sparkles on melting snow.

Whether lion or lamb, it's hard to know
when snowy piles are caked in grime.
March is here, let winter go.

One day warm, the next day cold
in uncertainty, we must abide.
Morning sun sparkles on melting snow.

No logic to how this month unfolds,
the weather snubs all reason and rhyme.
Still, March is here, let winter go.

Wait patiently for flowers to show
and save your shorts, it's not yet time.
Morning sun sparkles on melting snow.
March is here. Let's let winter go!

Four Haiku for April

Though the sky is grey,
this is a time of new birth.
New green is coming.

Watch for messages,
signs of the unexpected.
Stone, feather, cloud, wind.

Is it spring at last?
The robins do not worry,
each day, a gateway.

My house owns tulips
planted by another's hands.
Every spring, I smile.

Out at the Lighthouse

The lighthouse
holds fast to the concrete pad
at the end of the half-mile pier,
fire engine red against
four shades of water and sky.

Spring has come to Lake Michigan
and while there are no trees out this far,
if there were, you'd see new green
bursting from buds, tiny eruptions
lighting up the canopy.

But here, at the lake, it's just me, the pier,
and the lighthouse, a deaccessioned sentinel.
No longer guiding ships in, but inviting me out
to walk the gauntlet of white spray
as waves crash the break wall.

So, I go. I want to stand alone
way out at this terminus
where I will be met by nature's enormity.
Assuring myself there's no danger,
the conditions today are not that fierce.
But I am alone on this pier,
one false move and I could vanish.

Up the metal stairs with no banister I go,
scale around to the lake side and sit
with my back against the red column.
Clutching my notebook,
I scribble some lines,
hoping to hold onto these words
the wind works so hard
to pry from my hands.

Sheboygan Spring

Bristle branches sweep
mottled grey-white clouds across
a floor of blue sky.

Seize the day, they say.
What part should I hold? Clouds, sky
barren trees, cold ground?

So, we start again.
New month, new day, new sunshine,
nothing has been lost.

If there's a sameness
to every day, look for the
gift, the difference.

Today, cloud cover
blocks the sun's gift of light, warmth.
Still, I know it's there.

The birds sound happy.
Are they? Or do they complain
all day long, like us?

Cold, crisp, sunny day.
Bare trees etch poems on the sky.
I wish I spoke tree.

Everything After

Everything that happened
happened after
happily ever after.
Before now and then,
before time began
in a place we had forgotten.

Everything that was now
was in the ever after,
that ringing sound of laughter,
brittle voices in autumn sun.
Let's go, they said, *let's run
Down to the lake, it's fun.*

Time is only what we think.
Thirty years go by, just blink
and you will find yourself
right here where you started
just here where your heart is,
this place you never parted.

We could stand alone or not,
we could blossom, we could rot—
there is no rhyme or reason.
I only know that time stands still
when I hold your hand until
the coming of the season.

Ode to a Brat

Before I came here,
I did not know
that you rhyme
with *not*
and are not
a snotty child.
I did not know
they cook you
at a fry or grill out
(not a barbeque).
I did not know
of hard rolls,
fundraisers,
or soaked in beer.
I did not know
I could cross
Piggly Wiggly
parking lot
on any Saturday
to follow your scent
then eat you,
dear brat, before
heading home.

Acrostic for Ruth DeYoung Kohler

Riding in the family car on long ago Sunday afternoons,
Up and over the biggest bumps in the road, a young girl bloomed.
Trekking with her father in search of inspired bathtub shrines
He showed her the beauty in all things, making it all sublime.

Delight in meeting the makers, each encounter moved her ahead
Each artist a joy to know, beginning with Fred Smith who said,
You gotta have it in ya! An admonition she took to heart.
Outside of that, nothing can get done. And so, she saw her part.
Using her time and ingenuity, she made a plan to preserve the art of
Nohl, Tellen, Chand, Bowlin, Blagdon, Smith, EVB and more
Going all the miles to keep their work safe so new dreams can soar.

Kaleidoscope of wonderments she carried, seeking opportunity,
Opening new roads for artists to explore their art in industry.
How much rich creation sprang from her visionary sight?
Little would we know the possibilities without her shining light.
Every road has a goal, despite the bumps. She taught us that notion.
Ruth DeYoung Kohler, thank you for all you set in motion.

*At the request of the John Michael Kohler Arts Center for an activity at the Midsummer
Festival of the Arts, July, 2021*

Midsummer Serenade

A little wren went
gently on the breeze, flittered
up into the tree.

A day at the lake
wind on waves, sand in my shoes,
I ponder the clouds.

What makes a day good?
Gratitude for all the things.
Mostly, nectarines.

Out by the farm fields
lush green spreads far and wide. All
things are possible.

At dusk, the sky burns
pink, red, then orange. Then fireflies
spark and then, lightning.

Summer is just half
gone and already the thought:
we are nearly done.

50% Off Summer

The sign said, *the fun is over*
and everything is now worth
half of what it was at the beginning.

Sandals, towels, unguents
become meaningless in the face
of the coming north wind

that will soon deaden
all the thrills of summer:
warm nights by the fire pit

sunny mornings sleeping late.
There are beans to be picked
and pestos to be made.

There are more tomatoes
than you can shake a stick at,
and peaches, *ah, peaches.*

It's coming to an end here,
all the ripe possibilities of summer.
Despite all the warnings,

and even when nothing
particular happened,
summer's value still holds.

This Human Condition

As words come and go
they tell the miseries and joys
of this human condition.
What do we ever really know?

Through misery and joy
we live in community, still
what do we ever really know?
Can we change what's wrong?

We live in community, still
we hold fast to borders.
Can we change what's wrong,
make the world a better place?

We hold fast to borders,
but are born in our stories.
We can make the world a better place
for all that's at stake.

We are born in our stories
lifting memories and visions
of all that's at stake
for those yet to come.

Lifting memories and visions
to bring forth connection
for those yet come,
an abundance of grace.

Bring forth connection
as words come and go
an abundance of grace,
this human condition.

At the request of Mary Lynne Donohue for a gathering of the Wisconsin Humanities board of directors in Sheboygan, June 13, 2024

In Praise of Pollinators

Come forth,
you bees, you honey and bumble,
you pollen wasps and ants
you bee flies, hoverflies,
blowflies and mosquitoes.

Come forth, lepidopterans!
Yes you, butterflies and moths.
Also flower beetles,
bats and hummingbirds,
honeyeaters and sunbirds.

Let us not forget
monkeys, lemurs,
possums, and rodents.
You lizards, even you.
Everyone has a job to do.

Let us give thanks
to these creatures among us
destined to move pollen
from flower to flower
making our crops survive.

Let not one more day pass
that does not begin
in praise of pollinators.
To them, we owe the future.
Together, we will thrive.

Written for Friends of Peace Park for In Praise of Pollinators, August 29, 2021

In the Pick 'n Save Parking Lot

Looking over
the top of my mask
my glasses already steamed,
I meet your eyes, stranger,
and we smile.

We cannot see these smiles
but we know we are smiling.
The twinkle in the eye tells all.
We raise our hands in silent salute.

Nothing could have prepared us
for this moment, or maybe
everything did.
If only our hands could meet,
right here, we'd become a prayer.

We know we are members
of the same tribe,
fighting an insidious evil
that flourishes on the breath,
on the wind, and has run
unchecked in all the lies of now,
and in all the lies past.
Let it be unchecked no more.

In the journey towards justice,
there is just us, essential prophets
seeing beyond the mask.

Keeping House

I never really knew my house
until I lived inside all day, every day.

What used to be a rushing
to get to the next shiny place

has become a marathon of solitude
as I wait for bread to rise.

My heart beats in sync
with the ice maker in my fridge,

the sump pump in my basement,
and the ceiling fan above my head.

My bookshelves are sagging
under the weight of pending knowledge.

I have learned to measure time
by the angle of light on the floor.

How is it that once upon a time,
I ran around town, scattered

and maskless, breathing in
what everyone else breathed out?

Now, I sit in stillness, grateful
to earn my living from home,

privy to the persistence of mildew
and the advice of the air conditioner.

I have come to know doorknobs
and breadcrumbs, dead leaves fallen

from my house plants, and all
the maligned secrets of dust bunnies.

Sympathetic to the tea kettle's sorrow,
I bear witness to the confessions of my carpet.

I am not a better housekeeper,
just a better house knower.

The New House Reveals Itself

for M.D.

Winter rain on icy ground
and nothing prepared me
for pools of water everywhere,
my basement floor buckling.
What kind of membrane
am I living in? Permeable,
it seems. *Drain tile, the veins
and sump pump, the heart,*
said the weatherproofing man.

I did not know that a house
had a heart. I search daily
to find what muscle it is
that pumps life through
this structure that holds
my edges secure. Windows
for eyes, rooms for dreaming.
The kitchen, a fire in my belly,
the place where ideas are born.

Then comes a day in spring,
when tulips push through,
tulips planted by hands not mine.
I see a woman on her knees
in the grass, burying beauty
for some ingrate of the future.
But, no, I will not be that.
For, there, just there, I see it.
Tender tips of salmon red,
flamed with strokes of yellow.
The heart of the house,
making itself known to me.

Bodies of Water

We sit on the veranda at assisted living
looking across the fake pond at the trees.
Their reflections shiver as a breeze ripples
the murky surface of the water. You speak
of rivers and creeks and how all things
make their way to the sea.
I can't forget that everything in you
seeps from the cracks of your container
as dementia runs you through a wringer,
a towel hung to dry. You've seen it all
and share your cures in dainty spoonfuls.
Who benefits from this assisted living?
Guilt weighs heavy as sandbags
that shore up our old foundation.
I know the membranes we wear
only function when permeable.
I have no way of knowing where
one of us begins and the other ends.

Memory of My Father at the Lake

We were nearing the end of you.
You knew it, I knew it
but it was not something
we talked about.

We came down to this very shore
with sandwiches and a couple beers.
Looking out at the lake,
you said, *Let's make one more road trip.*
Knowing this would never happen,
I said, *Yes! Let's do it!*

Now it is sunrise and you,
seven years gone.
The lake calls me to remember,
gently undulates on and on.

An immense liquid mirror of the sky,
delivering a bridge to the sun,
reflecting you and me
and all of creation
in the wave of its hand.

All the Things

If flowers can bloom
and birds can sing,
then I can learn
to do anything.

I'll sew a button,
shine my shoe,
and every day,
learn something new.

Like ride a bike
or sail the sea,
climb a mountain,
climb a tree.

Bake some bread
or read a book.
I'll even write
my own. Just look!

If the sun can rise
and rain can fall,
then I can learn
to do it all.

Written for Poetry Day at Wilson School, 2021

Welcome, Sister!

Step up, step in!
Sheboygan awaits you.
Lakefront and City Green,
storefront and factory
art, music, commerce, cuisine.

The place where the waters meet,
the traditional homelands
of the Ho-Chunk,
Potawatomi, Menominee,
Oneida, and Ojibwe.

Join us to acknowledge
the indigenous peoples
still connected to this land.
Join us with waves of immigrants
who call this place home.

Step up, sit down!
For we are the city of chairs,
cheese, churches, and children.
Stroll (or dance!) along our streets
our boardwalks, our beaches.

Greetings dear Sister,
with joy, we welcome you.
Join us in planting this mighty oak,
to remind us of our connection,
our resilience and growth.

*Requested by Mayor Sorenson to welcome the delegates from Sheboygan's sister city,
Esslingen, Germany at a tree planting ceremony, July 3, 2023*

Investiture

We meet at this appointed time
to celebrate investiture.
All of us rejoice in this,
acknowledging your honor.

Empowered in this crucial task
to know and apply the law,
you'll instruct the jury to decide
from evidence they heard and saw.

You will listen and advise,
be reasonable and fair.
We know decisions that you make
are made with utmost care.

You wear the robe for all of us
and will not let the system fail.
With your wisdom on the bench
justice will prevail.

Requested by Judge Natasha Torry on the occasion of her investiture to the Sheboygan County Circuit Court-Branch 2, August 3, 2023

Paj Ntaub Maker

Even without eye glasses
she can set down perfect stitches

and make elaborate story cloths
to tell the tales of her people.

She made the Emperor's Daughter tale
and the Tiger tale. She made scenes

of daily life like the ball game, the harvest,
and crossing the Mekong River into Thailand

with babies silenced by a pinch of opium.
Such a long way to come, all the way

to Sheboygan, where I bought her cloth
at the farmer's market, and a bag of ripe tomatoes.

A Deer in the Evening Field

Night falls upon the oaks,
and I almost miss her,
my focus on the field
of wild carrot and milkweed,
the tangle of everything.

I feel a presence and there,
partially hidden by tall grass,
she stands, still as a statue.
She stares me down, the guardian
of this remnant forest. I stop.

There is a great distance
between us, and yet, our eyes lock.
Some would say she is the intruder.
She eats my tulips, they say.
But I know it's me who doesn't belong.

She studies me and I can see in her
all the deer hugging the roadside,
legs akimbo, bellies bloated,
almost peaceful. I want to apologize
for these houses that border her woods,

these busy roads that bring
cars and headlights. Nothing
a deer should be caught in.
She twitches her ear and I hope
she can hear me say, *I'm sorry.*

The First Day of School

As summer
comes to an end,
open books sing loud
their anthems, calling
the children to school.

More than new friends
or new shoes,
it is the summons
of empty notebooks
that promise

the fullness of paper
the pointedness of pencils,
the measure of rulers.
Whether caterpillars
into butterflies,

the lessons of history,
or sine and cosine,
knowledge awaits
the eager student
at the birth of every journey.

In uncertain moments,
the first day remains
the apple on the teacher's desk,
a classroom of young hearts
brimming with possibility.

For You

I'd like to write you a poem
to carry with you
Wherever you may roam
Something always true.

I'd like to sing you a song
A melody to fill your heart
And cheer you all day long
A tune to help you start.

I'd like to bake you a cake
A recipe rich and sweet
If you tell me what to make
I'll create that special treat.

I'd like to give you a gift
A gem to light your way
A boost to give you a lift
And make your lucky day.

A gift, a cake, a song, a poem
to keep you safe, to feel like home.

Written for Poetry Day at Wilson School, 2019

Eight Haiku for Autumn

Sun lights up the lake,
we walk through endless colors.
The dogs jump for joy.

My feet cut a path
through the weave of gold and brown.
The carpet whispers.

The world is singing:
wind soprano, geese alto
sky tenor, leaves bass.

Childhood memories,
lingering in piles of leaves.
Jump! And jump again.

Late walk by the lake,
so much blue sparked by yellow,
true meaning of life.

At this time of year
please give me a sweater vest.
Give me cinnamon.

Such jewels, fall leaves.
You'd think the tree would keep them,
knows it must let go.

Wild geese form a V
over the church parking lot.
Like us, heading home.

Six Haiku for November

Yesterday it snowed.
The tricksters stayed home, leaving
all the almond joy.

Things have gone icy,
the squirrels are on alert.
Time to hunker down.

One silent moment
to breathe, to dream, to listen,
to pause the tumult.

Leafless, silent trees
etch alphabets on the sky.
What are they saying?

Warm sun bathes my face.
Crisp, cool wind rustles dry leaves.
Spring in November!

If only one day
you find gratitude, then you
are missing the point.

Goods

The snowblower I want,
the one with the ice auger,

was ordered in October
but has not yet arrived.

I await the right tool
for when the snow plow comes

and leaves a pile of frozen snow
at the end of my driveway.

Supply chain disruptions
wreak havoc for each of us.

Goods are rendered useless
at ports from Long Beach to Savannah.

But then, there are goods
we can supply freely anytime.

Unspoken intangibles
that come in no container

a wave, a smile, a bundled neighbor
silently clearing the driveway.

The Moles in Winter

Icicles hang from the eave
above my front door,
malevolent daggers.
I am under house arrest,
held captive by winter.
I make another cup of tea
and await interrogation.

Will you ever seek public office?
If you were a sculpture, what pose would you take?
What do the words "true love" mean to you?

If only I had answers, I might escape this winter of my soul.

But look.
The moles are on the move.
See their tunnel networks
etched across the snowy lawn?
Their warm, furry bodies
push upward on the blanket of white.
If they can make an impression
in the dead of winter, so can I.
Underground, everything is possible.

In their ever-hopeful minds,
the moles know new life is coming.
Daggers be damned,
help is on the way.

Five Haiku for December

Fresh, crisp morning air,
the trees are down to bare bones.
The earth waits for snow.

Grateful for morning
cinnamon toast, cup of tea.
Remember these things.

Hard to be joyful
when everything is going
darker and darker.

Cold north wind blows hard,
stinging my fingers and face.
Please let's hurry home!

Come winter solstice!
Today we toggle the switch,
longer days ahead.

Sheboygan Sonnet: On the Occasion of the Lighting of the Tree

"The Christmas lights look like colored rain standing still."
–Laura Hogue Hartlep at age 9

We know with certainty, each day will end
we creatures who gather when darkness falls.
Mother, father, neighbor, child, and friend
we do what's right when loving kindness calls.
We walk this road together, wild and bleak
know in our hearts there is no other way.
Again, again, we turn the other cheek
bravely don the mask, small price to pay.
Witness now the trees, asking for our hands,
calling us to lighten their heavy boughs.
Awed by their gentle majesty we stand
to carry home this glow to every house.
Like colored rain stands still upon the pine,
each one of us, drops of light that shine.

At the request of Mike Vandersteen, Mayor of Sheboygan, 2013-2021, December 2020

If a City

If a city was a story,
it would begin long before
streets and structures.
It would begin with land
and proximity to water,
and people who lived there
before it was a city

If a city was a poem,
it would be spoken in slow,
meandering lines with a litany
of occurrences, triumphs,
missteps, and resolutions.
There would be growth,
and it would not always rhyme

If a city was a sentence,
it would be declarative.
It would have a noun, like neighbor
or friend and many verbs
igniting action: create,
discover, help, flourish,
dream, propose, remember

The adjectives in the city
would write themselves
and would be testimony
to all the good works
of the people who live there:
thriving, generous, just,
compassionate, and welcoming

There would be no period
at the end of the sentence, because
like a poem, the city is always
unfolding toward something better
and everyone who lives in that city
adds their voice to the story,
has a hand in its making

Requested by Contra-Tiempo Dance Theater, artists-in-residence at the John Michael Kohler Arts Center, for the film "What if a City," August, 2021

Acknowledgements

These poems, some in slightly different versions, first appeared in the following publications:

Everything After, *The Accidental Present*, Finishing Line Press, 2012

Ode to Brat, *Wisconsin Poets' Calendar*, 2014

50% Off Summer, *Your Daily Poem*, 2018

In the Pick 'n Save Parking Lot, *New Verse News*, 2020

Keeping House, *Verse Virtual*, 2022

The New House Reveals Itself, *Verse Virtual*, 2022

Bodies of Water, *Wisconsin People and Ideas*, 2024

Paj Ntaub Maker, *Wisconsin Poets' Calendar*, 2019

Haiku throughout this book appeared as individual poems in *5-7-5: a daily haiku journal*, Lone Snake Editions, 2024.

These poems first appeared in *Sheboygan Insider*, a monthly online publication of the mayor's office:

May Each One Flow

March Villanelle

Four Haiku for April

Acrostic for Ruth DeYoung Kohler

Midsummer Serenade

In Praise of Pollinators

Memory of My Father at the Lake

Welcome Sister!

A Deer in the Evening Field

The First Day of School

Six Haiku for November

Goods

The Moles in Winter

If a City

Sheboygan Sonnet: On the Occasion of the Lighting of the Tree

Books by Lisa Vihos

Poetry:

5-7-5: a daily haiku journal, Lone Snake Editions, 2024.

Fan Mail from Some Flounder, Main Street Rag Publishing, 2018.

This Particular Heaven, Kelsay Books, 2017.

The Accidental Present, Finishing Line Press, 2012.

A Brief History of Mail, Pebblebrook Press, 2011.

Fiction:

The Lone Snake: The Story of Sofonisba Anguissola, Water's Edge Press, 2022.

Anthologies:

From Everywhere a Little: A Migration Anthology, Water's Edge Press, 2019, Lisa Vihos and Dawn Hogue, editors.

Van Gogh Dreams, HenschelHAUS Publishing, 2018, compiled by Lisa Vihos.

100 Thousand Poets for Change: 10+ Years of Poetic Activism, Ediciones Anarca, 2023, Pilar Rodriguez Aranda, Lisa Vihos, Canuto Roldan, editors.